Marie-Josée Thibault

book 2

SAINT PATRICK SPEAKS

Saint Patrick Speaks - Book 2

Published by Abba Books LLC
abbabooksllc@gmail.com
Copyright © 2025 Marie-Josée Thibault

All Rights Reserved

No part of this publication may be reproduced, distributed, or transmitted in any form or by any means, including photocopying, recording, or other electronic or mechanical methods, without the prior written permission of the publisher.

First Edition, 2025
Designed and Edited by Abba Books LLC
ISBN: 978-1-967429-06-6

Abba Books LLC
34972 Newark Blvd, #441
Newark, CA 94560

www.abbamyfatheriloveyou.com
https://www.facebook.com/AbbaILoveYouBooks/

Thy Peace on Earth must be achieved. No light, no litany must be spared to honor Thy Grace.
-Saint Paul

TABLE OF CONTENT

Preface	VII	Chap 8	17	Chap 16	37
Chap 1	1	Chap 9	19	Chap 17	39
Chap 2	3	Chap 10	21	Chap 18	41
Chap 3	5	Chap 11	25	Chap 19	43
Chap 4	7	Chap 12	27	Chap 20	45
Chap 5	9	Chap 13	29	Chap 21	49
Chap 6	13	Chap 14	31	Chap 22	51
Chap 7	15	Chap 15	33	Chap 23	53
				Chap 24	55
				Chap 25	57
				Chap 26	59
				Chap 27	61

PREFACE

My children of this distressed Earth, listen to me carefully.

Saint Patrick is a logos of universal and divine teaching sourced from the Heart of Abba Father. This teaching is in continuity with the geographical and historical Ireland you know and the unique Spiritual Heritage it contains.

Saint Patrick fulfilled his mission to perfection, and the blessing bestowed by his grace onto Ireland is unique, powerful, universal, and—above all—rooted in love.

I bless you, and I love you.

Saint John Paul II

Saint Patrick Speaks

1 y friends, my children, listen to me carefully. It is true that the events to come will be difficult for everyone on Earth. Your faith in God will be your only shield of protection to survive the events to come. This is why it is imperative that you elevate your faith in God from today.

Repeat the prayer "Our Father" several times a day. Learn this prayer in Latin, the official language of Heaven, and repeat it often as well. Speak to the Father directly; speak to me and ask me to pray for you directly to the Father. Give your life to the Father completely and forever. The Father will be pleased with this. Christ is in you.

I love you.

Saint Patrick Speaks

2

My friends, my dear ones, listen to me carefully. It is impossible for me to tell you the precise date and time at which these events will begin. I can, however, tell you that if you read these lines, you will witness the Judgment of God.

These sacred lines are meant to support you and protect you during the global turbulence that will soon strike the entire Earth. Be strong and courageous. Pray without ceasing. Christ is in you.

I love you.

Saint Patrick Speaks

3 My friends, my children, listen to me well. Your heart is much greater than its physical dimensions show you and much more beautiful than your eyes perceive. Your heart, dear children, is the seat of your soul, and your soul is flooded with the Light of Christ, especially when you merge with all that Christ is: His Teaching, His Love, His Strength, His Passion, His Cross, His Redemption, and His Mercy.

Your heart becomes very big—it exceeds your physical body by several meters, and we are able to enter and exit your heart with more and more ease when it is open very wide to Christ. Do you see?

Open your heart to Christ and let Him make it so gigantic that Divine Providence can comfortably reside there. Christ is in you.

I love you.

Saint Patrick Speaks

4

My friends, my children of Earth, listen to me well. Nothing and no one can take away your faith—only you can. You are responsible for deepening your faith according to the directives of your own will; our influence in your life—that is, the influence of Divine Providence—is based on the inspiration we bring into your heart. Ultimately, the final decision to deepen your faith (or to lose it) is entirely yours. God the Father Almighty is watching you, loving you, protecting you, and directing the events of your life to awaken your consciousness to His Love and His Sovereign Presence towards all.

Sooner or later, you will return to Him; you decide through your own will the degree of human pain and misery that you are willing to burden yourself with, for the refusal of God's Love will inevitably make you unhappy, as well as the time to you waste needlessly before finally turning to Him for salvation. Christ is in you.

I love you.

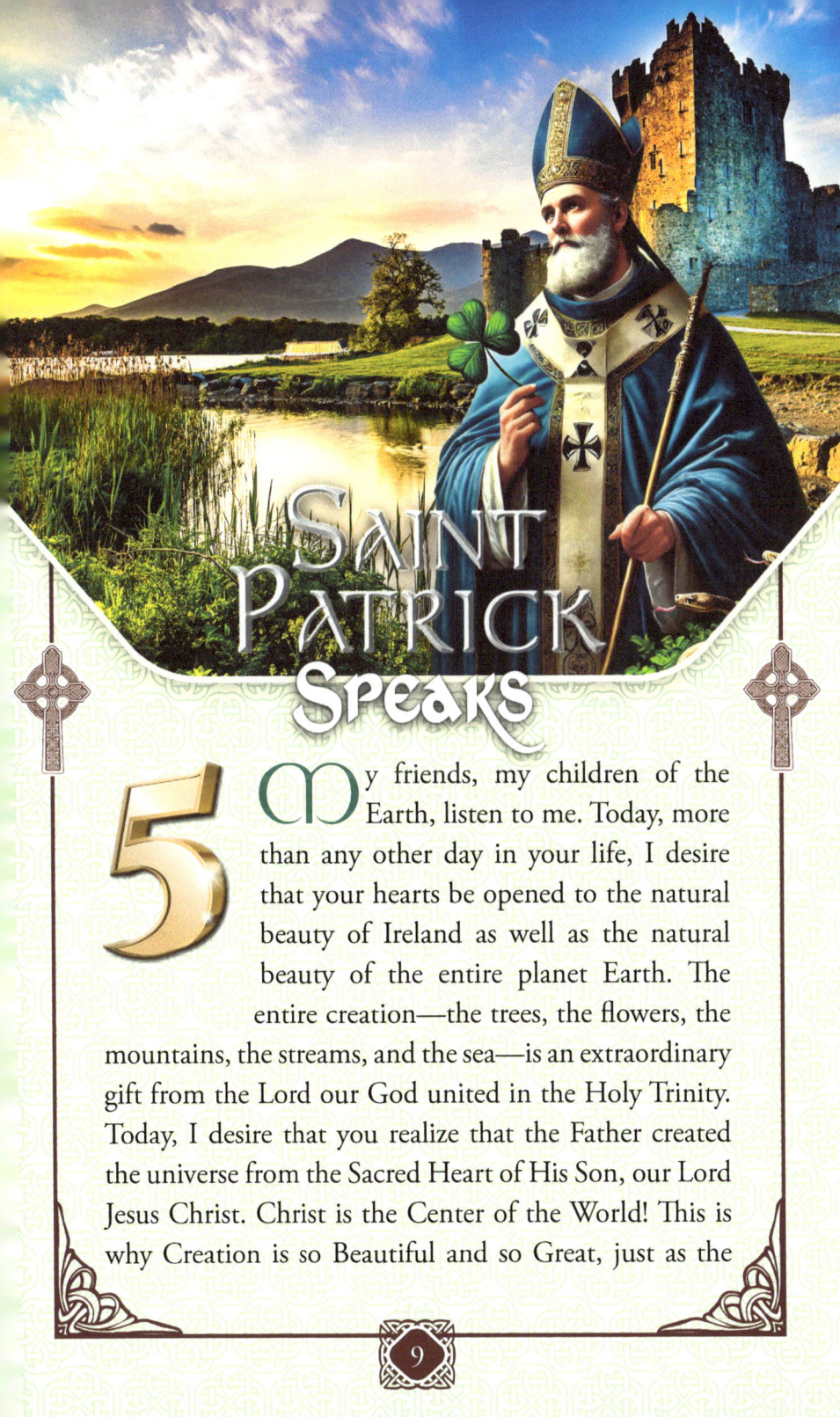

Saint Patrick Speaks

5 My friends, my children of the Earth, listen to me. Today, more than any other day in your life, I desire that your hearts be opened to the natural beauty of Ireland as well as the natural beauty of the entire planet Earth. The entire creation—the trees, the flowers, the mountains, the streams, and the sea—is an extraordinary gift from the Lord our God united in the Holy Trinity. Today, I desire that you realize that the Father created the universe from the Sacred Heart of His Son, our Lord Jesus Christ. Christ is the Center of the World! This is why Creation is so Beautiful and so Great, just as the

Christ is in you,
and we love you
so much!

~ Saint Patrick

Sacred Heart of Christ is so Beautiful and so Great... Do you see?

    Honor and thank the Father for His extraordinary Creation, and in the same breath of prayer, honor and thank the Sacred Heart of His Son, the Source of all. Christ is in you.

    I love you.

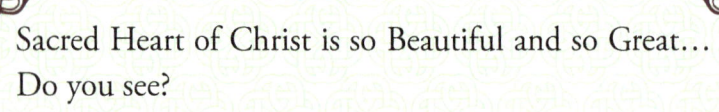

Saint Patrick Speaks

My friends, my children of Earth, listen to me carefully. It is clear to me—as well as to all the inhabitants of Paradise—that the Father loves you. Oh, how much He loves you! Look at the beauty of nature that surrounds you! Look at the beauty and functionality of the human body, which the Father Himself created! Look at all the comforts of modern life that the Holy Spirit has brought about through Its creative inspiration! Look around you and know that everything around you was permitted and willed by God the Father and none other than God the Father.

Let us give God the Father, the Creator of us all, a beautiful, great, and profound thanksgiving for all His Blessings. Christ is in you.

I love you.

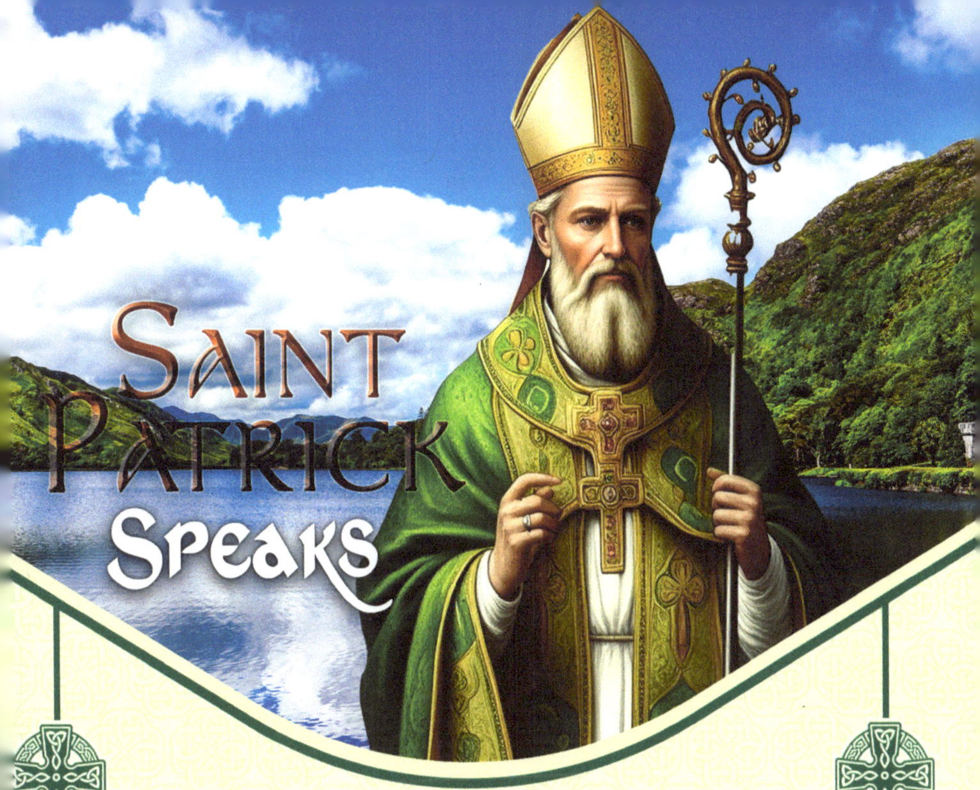

Saint Patrick Speaks

7

My friends, my children of Earth, listen to me carefully.

It is impossible for me to hide the truth from you: Heaven has opened for you and will never close. Do not neglect this gift from God, this gift born of His Divine Mercy, this richness found nowhere else on Earth. This is the Truth that is truer than the floor that supports you, the house that shelters you, and the food that satisfies your hunger. My presence in your life is truer than everything around you that is tangible and visible.

I say unto you, I say unto you verily: My presence in your life is true, and my providential influence—and that of the other Saints in Paradise—will increase from day to day , for this is the Will of God, the Almighty Father who adores you. Christ is in you.

I love you.

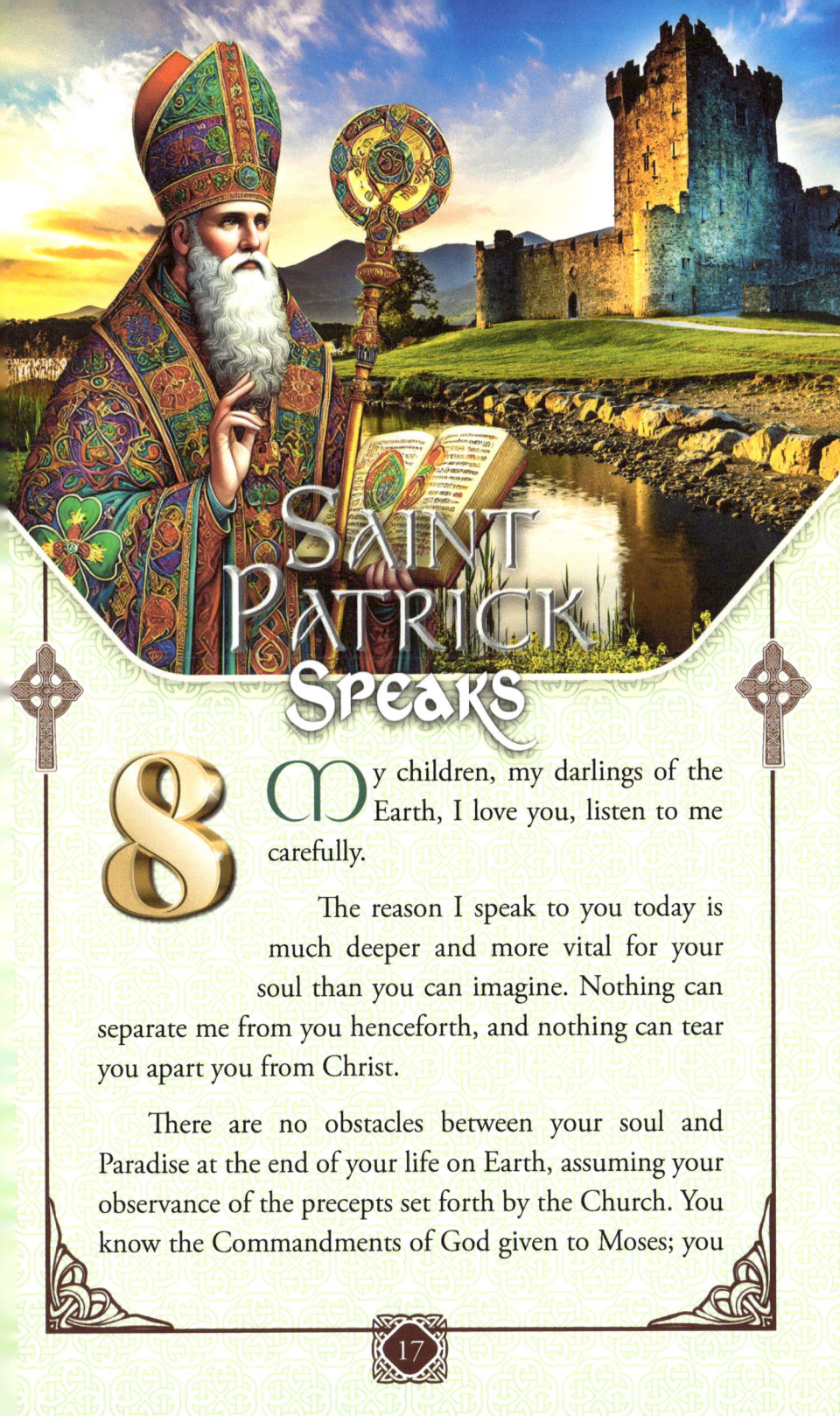

Saint Patrick Speaks

8 My children, my darlings of the Earth, I love you, listen to me carefully.

The reason I speak to you today is much deeper and more vital for your soul than you can imagine. Nothing can separate me from you henceforth, and nothing can tear you apart you from Christ.

There are no obstacles between your soul and Paradise at the end of your life on Earth, assuming your observance of the precepts set forth by the Church. You know the Commandments of God given to Moses; you know the Teachings of Christ as described in the Bible; you know the preachings of the Prophets of the Old Testament; you know the miraculous apparitions of the Virgin Mary throughout the world; and you know the Saints of humanity who have testified in their own way to the holy virtues of Christ in their lives.

Now, starting today, it is up to you to devote yourself completely to God according to the promptings of the Holy Spirit in your heart. Christ is in you.

I love you.

Saint Patrick Speaks

9 My friends, my children of the Earth, listen to me carefully.

Today, listen to nothing you hear with your ears, look at nothing you see with your eyes, and believe nothing you feel with your sense of touch. Life as you imagine, as you live in this temporal world, does not exist.

All that exists is your soul interacting with us, speaking to Christ Jesus and the Virgin Mary, praying to God, seeing the Angels bustling around you and the Paradise that awaits you after the passage that is death.

Today, listen only with your heart. Look only with the eyes of the heart and feel our closeness at the level of your heart, for our reality, here near you and there in the afterlife, is truer than your temporal world. As the heart is the seat of the soul, the heart is where I desire to see you live. Christ is in you.

I love you.

Saint Patrick Speaks

10

My friends, my children of the Earth, listen to me carefully. Today, look at your life so far: the beautiful and the ugly, the good and the bad, the greatness and the shortcomings. Now, imagine that you are rolling all of this into a ball of paper in your hands and throwing it as far away from you as you can, for today, you are starting anew!

From now on, you will walk in the Holy Footsteps of Christ, illuminated by the Light of the Holy Spirit who will show you the way, supported by the Sovereign

I stand before you at this moment as you read these lines.

~ Saint Patrick

Power of the Father, protected by your Guardian Angel, and assisted by me, Saint Patrick of Ireland, and all the Saints in Heaven as well as the Angels of God. God has decided this Divine Plan for your soul today. Christ is in you.

    I love you.

Saint Patrick Speaks

11

My children, my friends on Earth, listen to me carefully. This life you were given will be taken back very soon. Life is so short! Don't waste a single minute on the small details of your life—or even the big details, in fact.

Don't waste precious time making life plans that don't consider God's will, and don't let your mind wander over past dramas or conversations that will never return.

Always remain in the present moment with me, Saint Patrick of Ireland; with all the Saints in Heaven who love and guide you; with your Guardian Angel, who protects you, with Christ Jesus our Lord who saves you at every moment of your life; with the Virgin Mary, our Divine Mother who loves you tenderly; with the Holy Spirit, the Spirit of God the Comforter; and with God the Father Almighty, who is Love and Forgiveness to all. Christ is in you.

I love you.

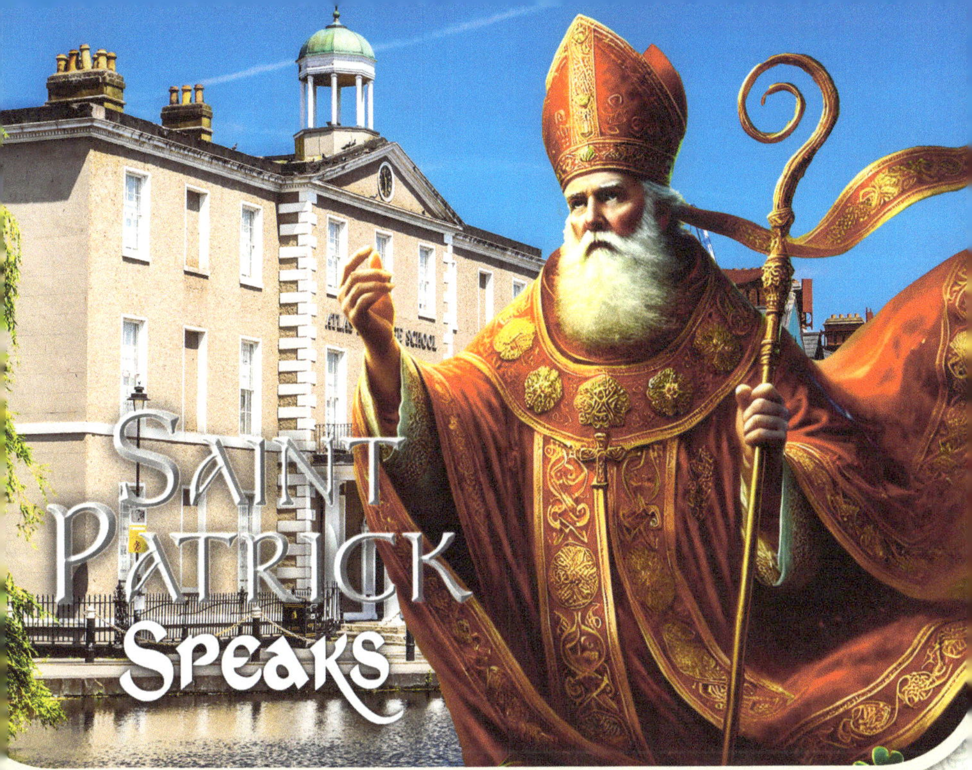

Saint Patrick Speaks

12 My friends, my children, listen to me carefully. Today, Christ the Lord our God makes you share in His suffering on the Cross, and He gives you the Key to Holiness. Place yourself in front of a large Cross.

Adore the Cross that Christ carried for our sins as well as His Merciful Wounds. Say an Our Father.

Turn around and place your back towards the Cross and cross your arms. Imagine the nails of the crucifixion passing through your own hands and feet and imagine the crown of thorns on your head. Say another Our Father. What do you see? What do you feel?

All suffering experienced in the Name of the Father, for His Glory and for His Love, is sweet in His Eyes and makes the soul beautiful, great, and white as snow. Here is the Key to Holiness. Learn to offer to God every bit of pain and suffering that life brings you, for the primary and initial purpose behind the pain you are experiencing, according to God's plan for you, is the ultimate sanctification of your soul. Christ is in you.

I love you.

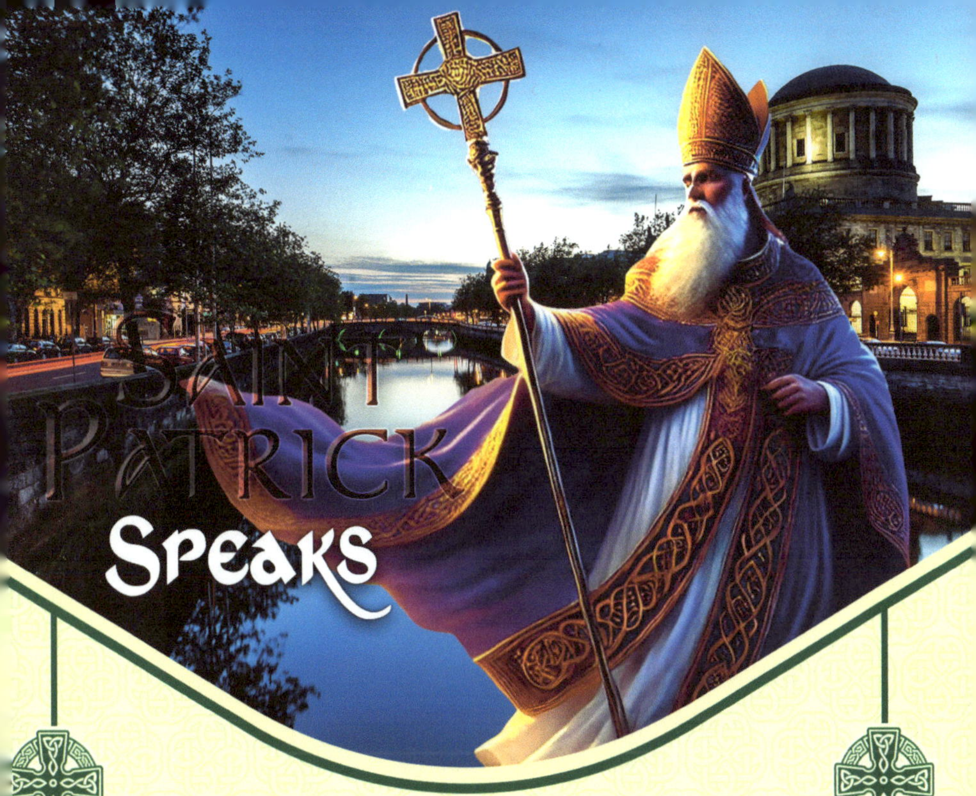

Saint Patrick Speaks

13

My children, my friends on Earth, listen to me carefully. Give to me the troubles of yesterday, the troubles of today, the troubles of tomorrow, and your entire life on Earth. The hearts that surround you, your living environment, your work, and your daily life: give them to me. Your questions, your dilemmas, your hopes and your despairs: give them to me. Your emotions, your thoughts, your spiritual life, and your life after death: give them to me. Your decisions, your affirmations, your beliefs, and above all your faith: give them to me.

Give everything to me, as well as to Christ Jesus our Lord and our God, and all of Heaven will take charge of your life on Earth, and it will be flooded with miracles and blessings! Christ is in you.

I love you.

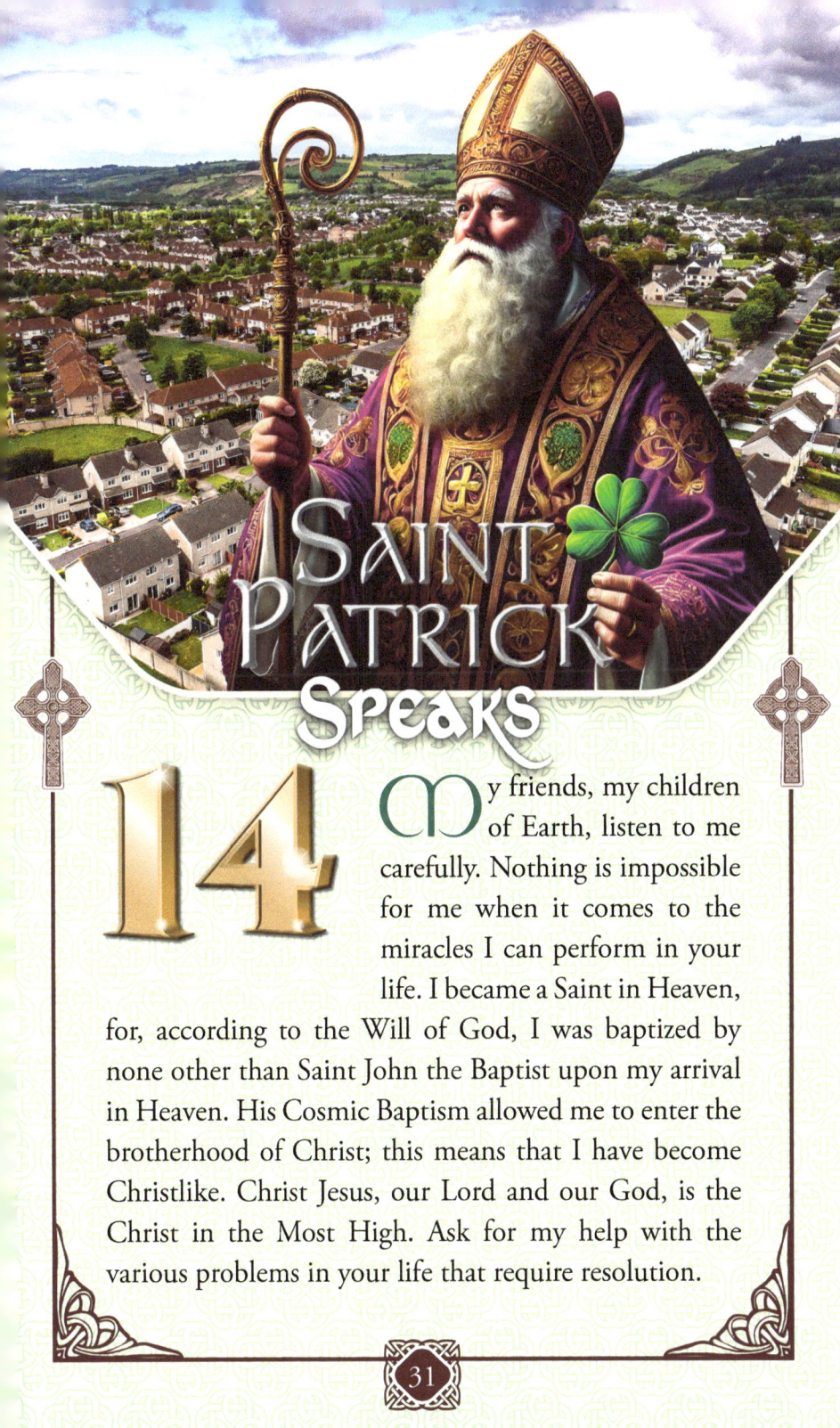

Saint Patrick Speaks

14

My friends, my children of Earth, listen to me carefully. Nothing is impossible for me when it comes to the miracles I can perform in your life. I became a Saint in Heaven, for, according to the Will of God, I was baptized by none other than Saint John the Baptist upon my arrival in Heaven. His Cosmic Baptism allowed me to enter the brotherhood of Christ; this means that I have become Christlike. Christ Jesus, our Lord and our God, is the Christ in the Most High. Ask for my help with the various problems in your life that require resolution.

Repeat this often: "Saint Patrick of Ireland, intercede for me before God the Father Almighty, so that I may obtain [requested favor] by virtue of your gift of responsibility of the Spiritual Heritage, through the Holy and Blessed Name of Our Lord Jesus Christ and the Immaculate Heart of Mary. Amen." Christ is in you.

I love you.

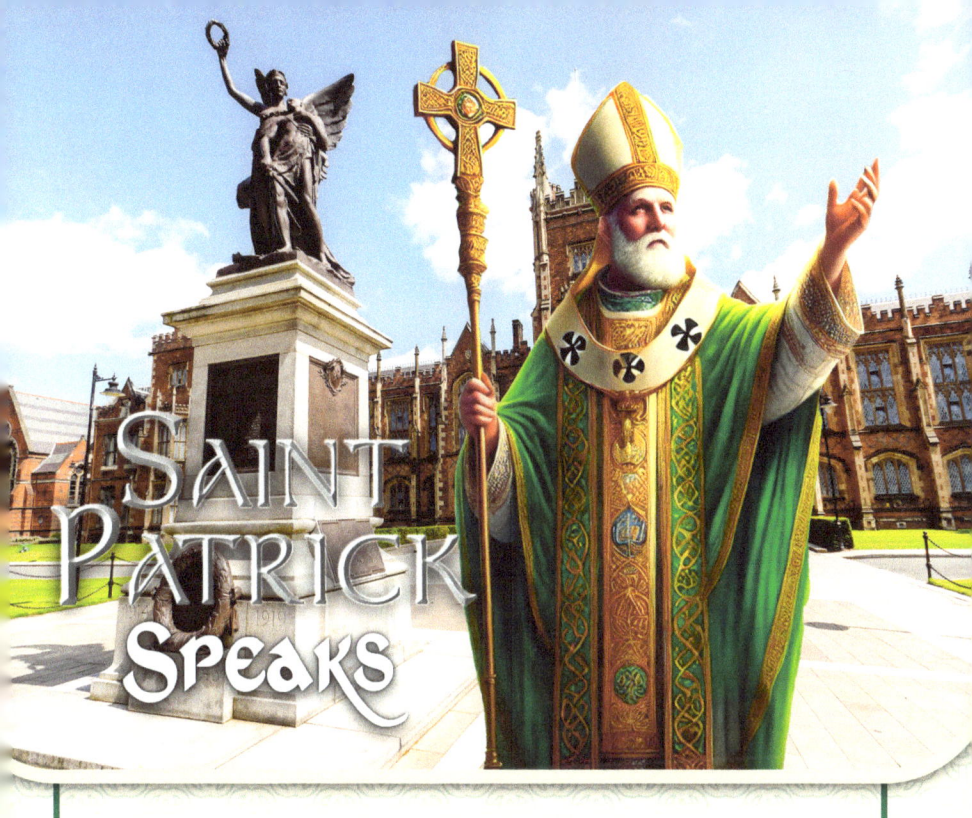

Saint Patrick Speaks

15

My children, my friends on Earth, listen to me carefully. It is impossible for me to explain the indescribable joy that fills me when I am able to speak to you. What exhilaration! What a blessing! What God's Mercy!

We, the Saints in Paradise, are much more than faces on holy pictures and names inscribed on pages explaining our previous lives on Earth. We are all alive and well in Paradise, and we are all alive in the same way on Earth—albeit in a dimension unknown to humans.

Love the Blessed Virgin Mary and all of Heaven will rejoice.

~ Saint Patrick

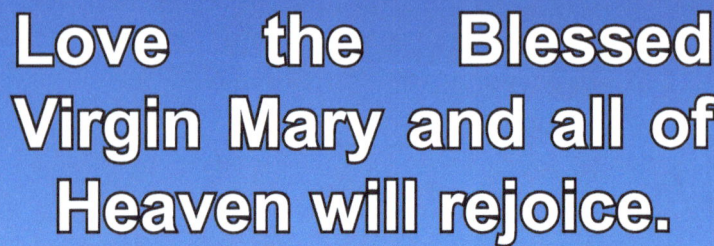

We move among you, interact with you, inspire you, and comfort you far more often than you can imagine.

Glory to God in the highest for granting so much Mercy upon your lives! Amen. Alleluia!

I love you.

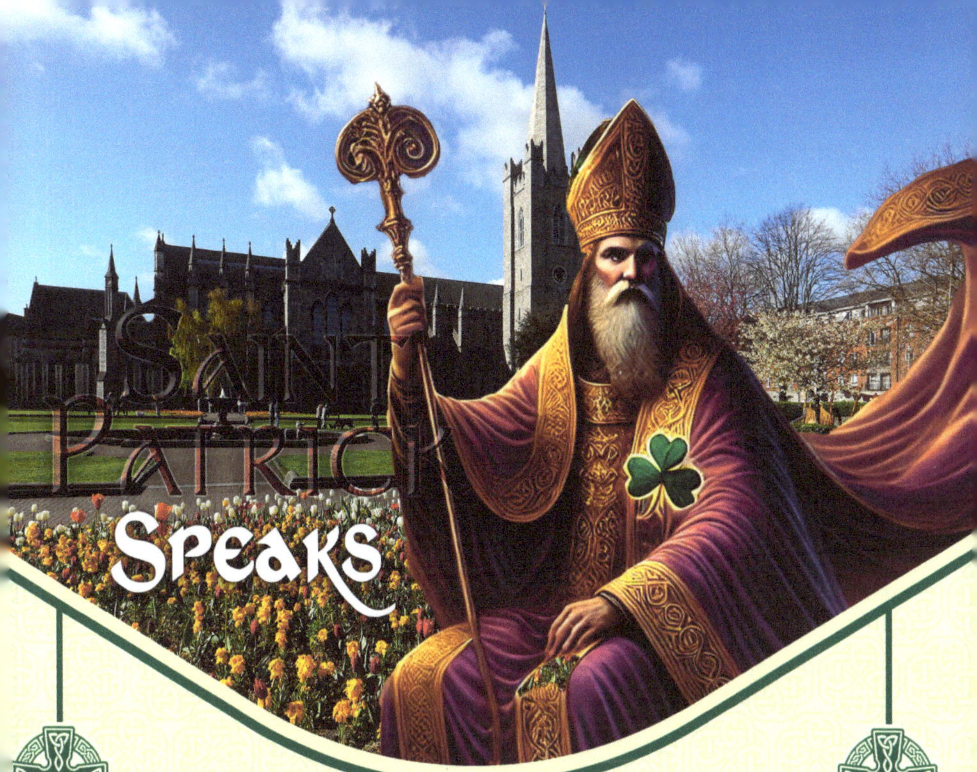

Saint Patrick Speaks

16

My friends, my children of the Earth, listen to me carefully. I love you no matter your past, no matter how your life is today, and no matter what happened just a few minutes ago.

I love you no matter if your faith is shaky, if your prayers are inconsistent, or if you are not fully attentive during your visits to Church.

I love you no matter if you don't read the Bible every day, if you forget to make the sign of the Cross, or if you have moments of anxiety or anger.

I love you, Jesus loves you, the Virgin Mary loves you, your Guardian Angel loves you, all of Heaven loves you, the Holy Spirit loves you, and above all, God the Father Almighty loves you. Christ is in you.

I love you.

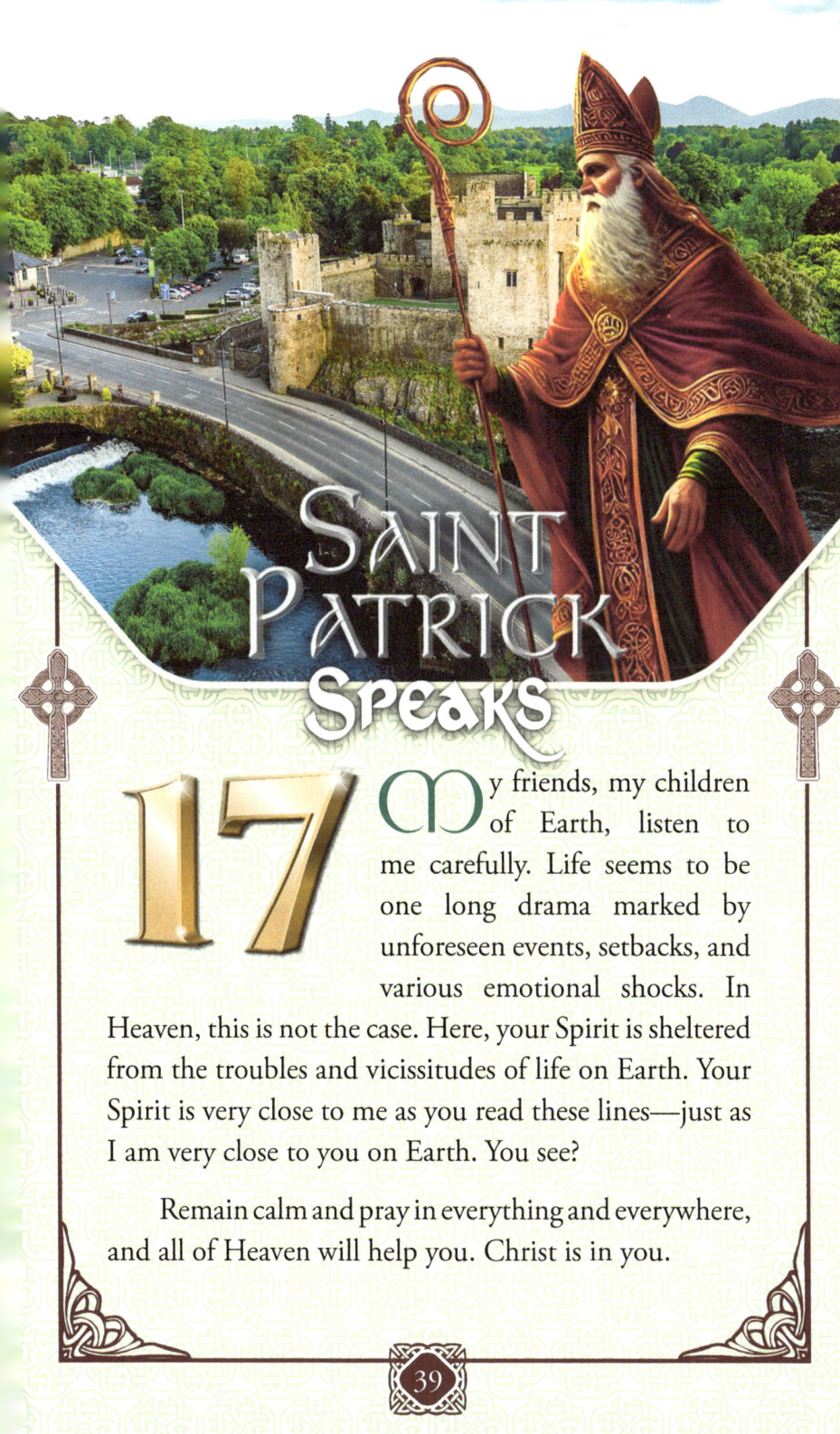

Saint Patrick Speaks

17

My friends, my children of Earth, listen to me carefully. Life seems to be one long drama marked by unforeseen events, setbacks, and various emotional shocks. In Heaven, this is not the case. Here, your Spirit is sheltered from the troubles and vicissitudes of life on Earth. Your Spirit is very close to me as you read these lines—just as I am very close to you on Earth. You see?

Remain calm and pray in everything and everywhere, and all of Heaven will help you. Christ is in you.

I love you.

Saint Patrick

Saint Patrick Speaks

18

My friends, my children of Earth, listen to me carefully.

There is nothing more important in your life than your personal and intimate relationship with God the Father, who has sent you many Messengers throughout history: His Beloved Son, our Lord Jesus Christ; the Most Holy Virgin Mary, Our Divine Mother; the Prophets and Apostles; and the Saints of the Earth, who now live together in Paradise.

I, Saint Patrick of Ireland, your friend and a

Messenger from Heaven, invite you to live and share the Good News of the Kingdom of God.

I say unto you, I say unto you verily: there is nothing more important than your personal and intimate relationship with God the Father Almighty.

Christ is in you.

I love you.

Saint Patrick Speaks

19

My friends, my children of the Earth, listen to me carefully.

Life on Earth is filled with unforeseen events, setbacks, and incidents of all kinds. The key to holiness during one's time on Earth is to always return to the Source of Life: our Lord Jesus Christ. Remember the Cross he carried with so much courage and love and recall how much injustice and ingratitude there is toward Him! How much cruelty and wickedness is hurled toward Him! How much hatred and jealousy is present in the hearts that have sinned against Him!

Remember that Christ's mission was to obey and fulfill the Father's will on Earth through both the suffering He endured and the miracles He performed in the Name of the Father.

Therefore, carry your cross—the one the Father will give you—in the Name of Christ the Savior, and the Father will be pleased. Christ is in you.

I love you.

Saint Patrick Speaks

20

My friends, my children of the Earth, listen to me carefully.

I have never been given the opportunity to speak to you until now. Oh, how I have longed to speak to you for such a long time! I carry Ireland, and the whole world, in the depths of my Divine Heart, and I desire with all my might to see your soul become beautiful, great, and white in the Eyes of God.

I will now atell you about my life on Earth.

My childhood in England was very happy and spent

The Divine Mercy bestowed by my holy presence cannot be estimated by the human intellect.

~ Saint Patrick

among my Christian family. However, pagan Ireland at the time was a dangerous enemy because of the kidnappings to which we were subjected.

You cannot imagine the horror of being captured and forced into slavery.

I will continue my speech shortly.

Christ is in you. I love you.

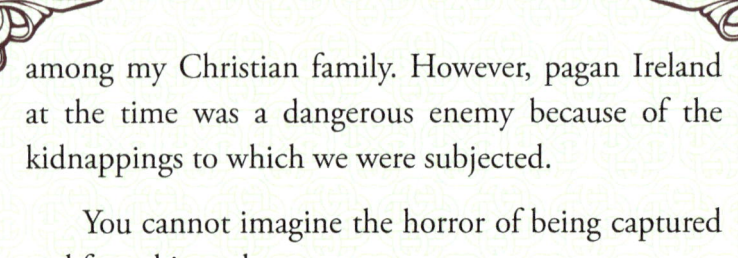

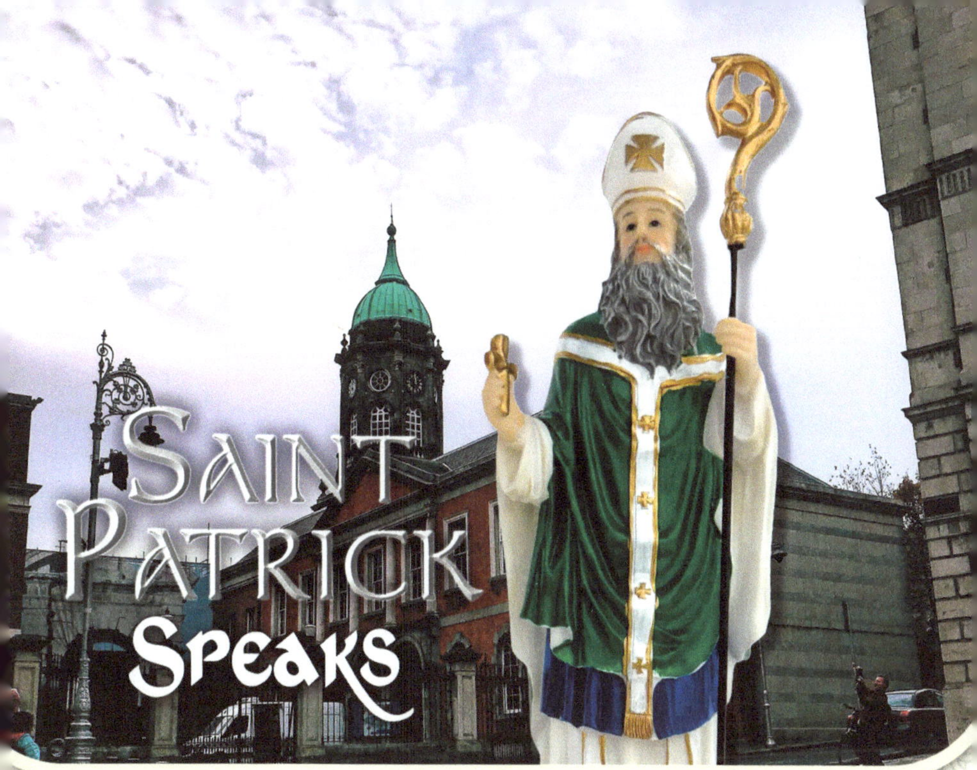

Saint Patrick Speaks

21

My friends, my children, listen to me carefully.

My enslavement was a critical period of profound and radical transformation at the level of my soul. I was a typical teenager, frivolous and mundane. I became a young adult anchored and strong in the Christian faith through this trial.

God the Father had wisely planned this extraordinarily difficult period for me to bring about my complete transformation. God's plan is always crowned with success!

I say this unto you, I say this unto you verily: God has a plan for you, and He will reveal it to you very soon.

Christ is in you. I love you.

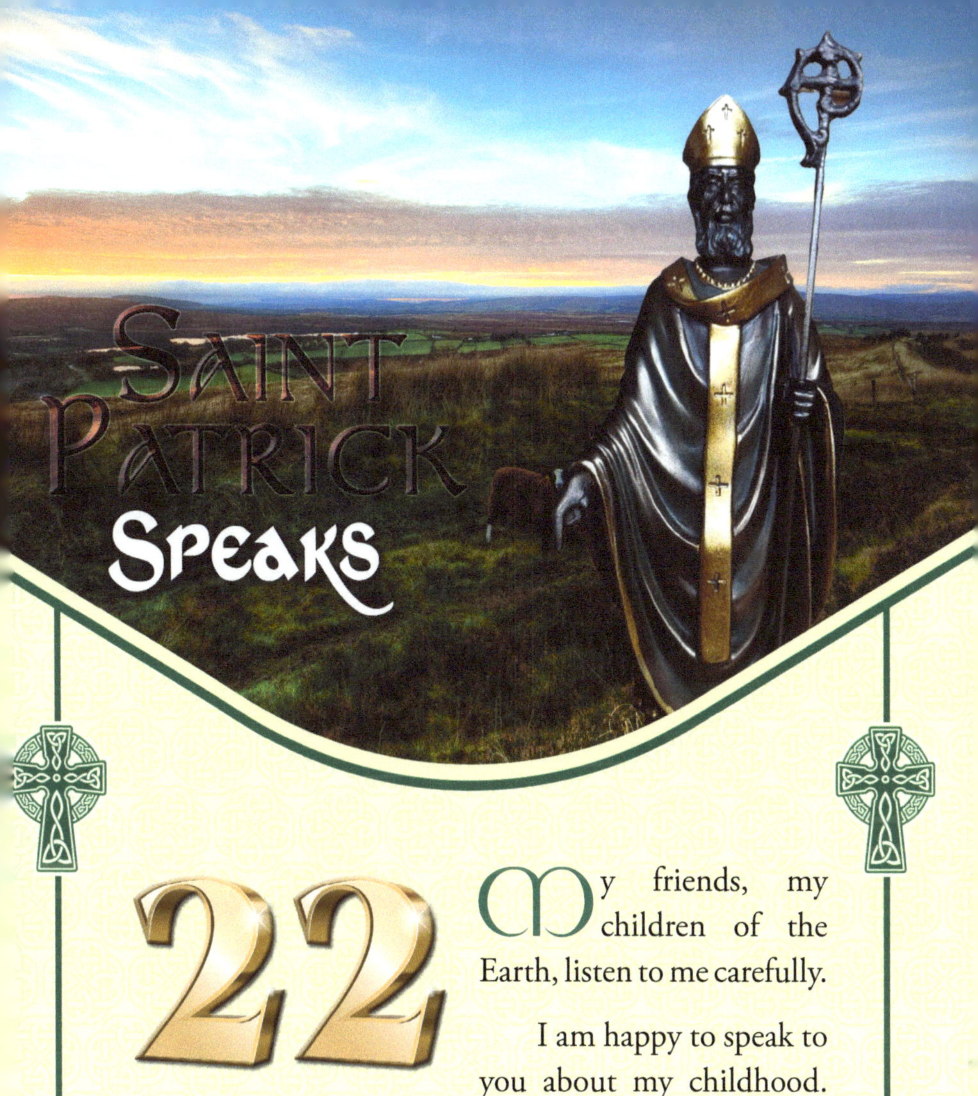

Saint Patrick Speaks

22

My friends, my children of the Earth, listen to me carefully.

I am happy to speak to you about my childhood. When I was little, my parents introduced me to Christianity and the precepts of the Church.

During my slavery, I gave my body and soul to God through Christ by structuring my days and devoting my time to prayer and reading the Bible I obtained. Little by little, the Christian teachings I received as a child grew firmer and stronger within me, as I relied on them to overcome the horrors of slavery.

Glory to God in the Highest Heaven, and peace on Earth to men of good will! Amen! Alleluia! Christ is in you. I love you.

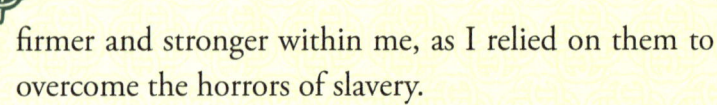

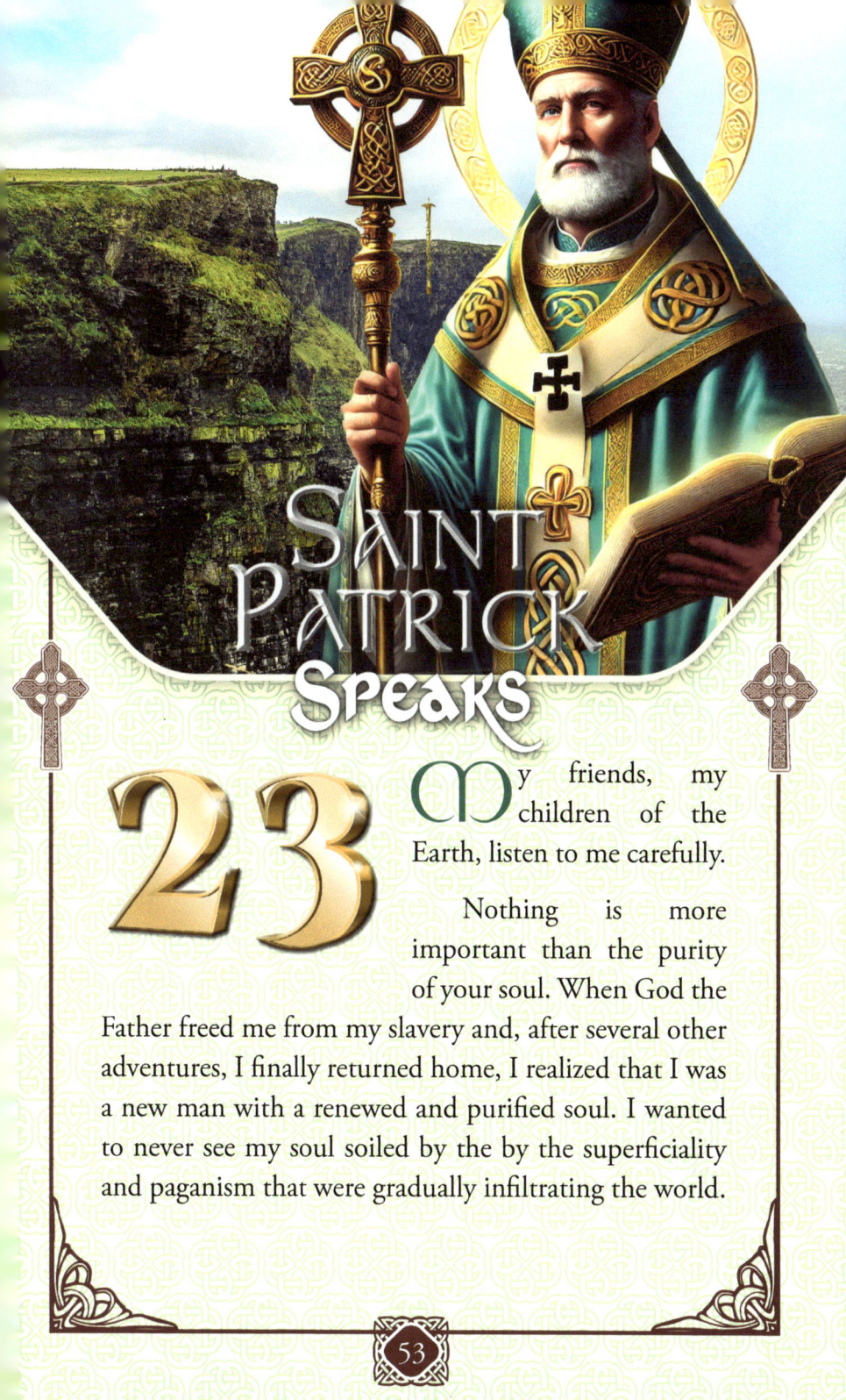

Saint Patrick Speaks

23

My friends, my children of the Earth, listen to me carefully.

Nothing is more important than the purity of your soul. When God the Father freed me from my slavery and, after several other adventures, I finally returned home, I realized that I was a new man with a renewed and purified soul. I wanted to never see my soul soiled by the by the superficiality and paganism that were gradually infiltrating the world.

I desperately desired to draw even closer to God to strengthen my soul even more and to make it beautiful and great like Christ and for the Father to all. I wanted to share the Good News of the Kingdom of God. The Father answered my prayers and helped me become a priest, and I was soon on my way back to Ireland. Christ is in you.

I love you.

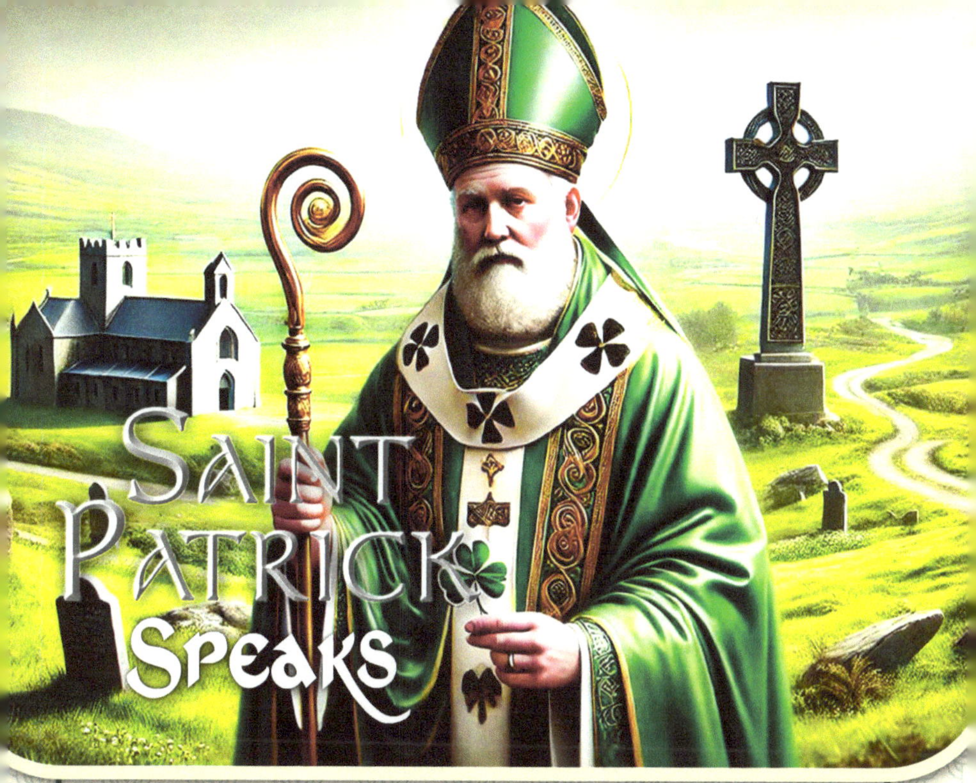

24

My friends, my children of the Earth, listen to me carefully.

My return to Ireland was filled with unexpected adventures. My colleagues in the clergy were unsympathetic to my missionary aspirations and religious fervor. I also encountered many obstacles from the druids and pagan attitudes that had been in place for hundreds of years.

God the Father comforted me, strengthened me,

protected me, and guided me throughout the trials He sent my way.

Little by little, the Catholic religion took root in the hearts and parishes of my beloved Ireland. Glory to God in the Highest, and Peace on Earth to men of goodwill! Amen! Christ is in you.

I love you.

Saint Patrick Speaks

25

My friends, my children of the Earth, listen to me carefully.

It is impossible for me to explain how much I love you. Oh, how I love you! I love you even more than I loved the Ireland of old, even more than the souls the Father entrusted to me for their conversion during my stay on Earth, even more than I loved living the apostolic mission God gave me at that time. I love you even more now because my human heart has been changed upon my entry into Paradise into a Divine Heart by the Grace of God and His Infinite

Mercy upon my sinful soul.

Glory to God in the Highest Heavens!

I make this my prayer: "May your human heart be changed into a Divine Heart after the passage that is death."

Christ is in you. I love you.

Saint Patrick Speaks

26

My friends, my children of Earth, listen to me carefully.

Nothing on Earth should attract your attention. Nothing on Earth should occupy your thoughts or emotions to the point that you are obsessed or frightened. Nothing on Earth will survive unless God the Father so decides.

Sail on the waves of your life with one foot on Earth and one foot in Heaven with us.

Everything will then be illuminated with a clarity, a

Love, and a Peace of divine origin that is far more real, powerful, and permanent than the shadows, the voids, and the dramas of life on Earth.

Pray! Pray! Pray! And cherish these moments spent with us, the inhabitants of Heaven, for if you honor the treasures that reside here on Earth, then your heart will be here too, now, tomorrow, and after the passage that is death. Christ is in you.

I love you.

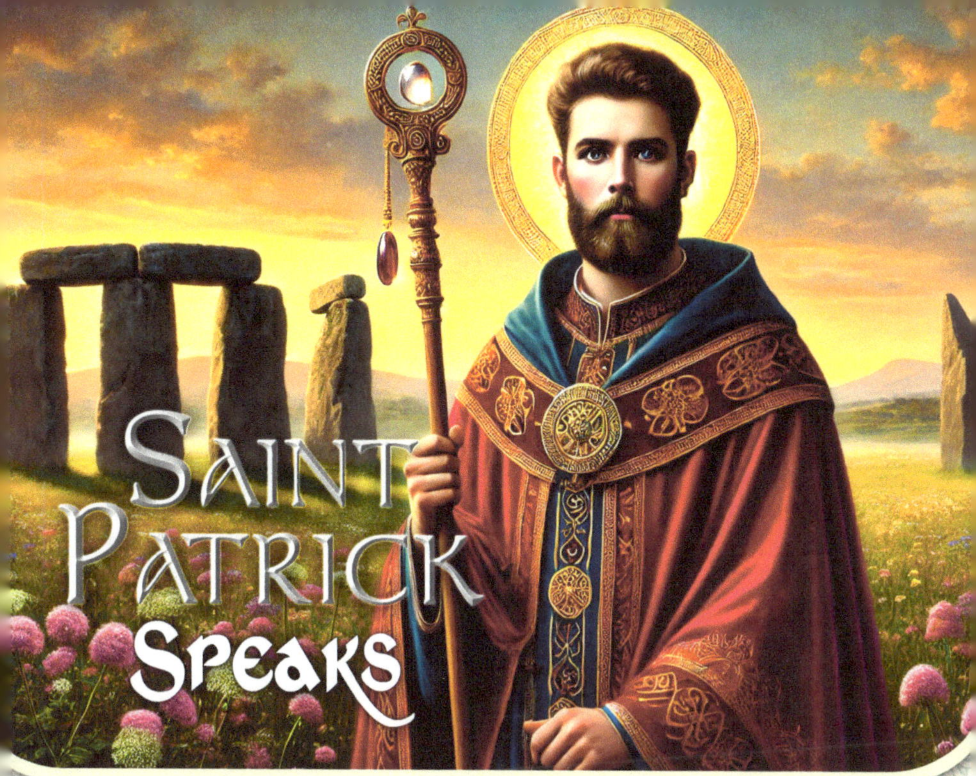

Saint Patrick Speaks

27 My friends, my children of the Earth, listen to me carefully. I am coming to the end of my presentation. I will speak to you again soon. Always and in everything, be firm in your faith. I will always be with you.

Repeat this often: "Saint Patrick, guardian of the Catholic Spiritual Heritage, pray for us."

Christ is in you. I love you.

Saint Patrick of Ireland

AFTERWORD

Saint Patrick and I are holding your hands as you read these lines. We await you at the Gates of Paradise after the passage that is death.

I bless you and I love you.

Saint John Paul II

Marie-Josée Thibault's life is in no way similar to yours. When she wakes, the saints of Heaven visit her, talk to her, teach her, and pray intensely with her. When such mystical sessions draw to a close, she greets with great respect and deep reverence the Masters of the Heavenly Court. This servant of the Lord spends the rest of the day in the company of her guardian angel, who continues her spiritual education and ceaselessly protects her from the perils of this fallen world.

Bestowed by the Heavenly Father, her gifts of clairvoyance and clairaudience allow her to remain in continuous contact with the supernatural dimension juxtaposed with ours, where the soul is born of the Spirit through Jesus and Mary. She prays that, one day soon, the entire human race will give glory to the Father, the Son, and the Holy Spirit.

ABOUT THE AUTHOR

ALSO BY THE AUTHOR

- Abba, Your Father, Speaks: Book I
- Abba, Your Father, Speaks: Book II
- Abba, Your Father, Speaks: Book III
- Abba, Your Father, Speaks: Book IV
- Dear Humanity: Book 1
- Dear Humanity: Book 2
- Dear Humanity: Book 3
- St Therese of Lisieux Speaks - Book 1: I Am The Heart of the Rose
- Saint Francis of Assisi Speaks - Book 1
- Saint Francis of Assisi Speaks - Book 2
- Saint Martin de Porres Spaeaks - Book 1
- Saint Bernadette Speaks - Book 1
- Saint Joan of Arc Speaks - Book 1
- Saint Padre Pio Speaks: Book 1
- Saint Padre Pio Speaks: Book 2
- Saint Padre Pio Speaks: Book 3
- Saint Beethoven Speaks - Book 1
- Saint Barnabas Speaks - Book 1
- Angel Gabriel Speaks: Book 1
- The Holy Pope Saint John Paul II Speaks - Book 1
- The Holy Pope Saint John Paul II Speaks - Book 2
- Prophet Moses Speaks 1
- Saint John the Baptist Speaks

www.ingramcontent.com/pod-product-compliance
Lightning Source LLC
Chambersburg PA
CBHW041627220426
43663CB00001B/31